God made the
MARSH

MIKE ATNIP

ISBN: 978-1-941213-94-0

Cover photo: Mike Atnip

All photographs in this book are by Mike and Daniel Atnip, with the following exceptions:

Virginia rail, page 25: Wikipedia User: Cephas CC BY-SA 3.0 (https://creativecommons.org/licenses/by-sa/3.0/legalcode).

Beaver, page 37: istockphoto.com

Bald eagle, page 42: public domain

Most of the photos were taken in the Killbuck Marsh Wildlife Area and the Lower Killbuck Creek Wildlife Area in Holmes and Wayne Counties, Ohio.

Printed in India

Published by:
TGS International
P.O. Box 355, Berlin, Ohio 44610 USA
Phone: 330-893-4828 | Fax: 330-893-2305 | www.tgsinternational.com

TGS001178

Some people think marshes are ugly and worthless. Does this look like a pretty place to you?

Would you like to explore the marsh and see what God has hidden there?

Good, let's go! Grab your binoculars, magnifying glass, and some lunch; then jump into the canoe with us.

Wait, let's not paddle yet. Did you see that buttonbush over on the right? God designed the buttonbush to survive in flooded places. Deer eat its leaves and bees sip nectar from the flowers.

I wonder how a cattail got its name. This one reminds me of a rat tail.

Ah, let's watch the honeybee suck nectar out of this flower. The bee will take the nectar home to make some sweet honey. Thank God for honeybees!

Each dead tree with its straggly limbs has its own beauty and story. Do you see the hole in one tree? I wonder if a tree swallow makes its home there.

9

Somebody is watching us down there. I'm glad my eyes don't bulge like this frog's eyes!

I wonder if those little algae pieces taste good. It would be hard to swim here without getting some in your mouth.

Shhh, I think the muskrat
sees us too. He seems to be
eyeing us as he heads home.
Muskrats love marshes.

I am sure that spider sees us as well. See how it is trying to stretch out and hide on the twig? We almost missed it. The small animals are important to the life of the marsh.

Use your binoculars to look at the painted turtle on the log. Move slowly, because turtles can see well and will quickly slide into the water if they notice us. I would hate to get scratched by those claws!

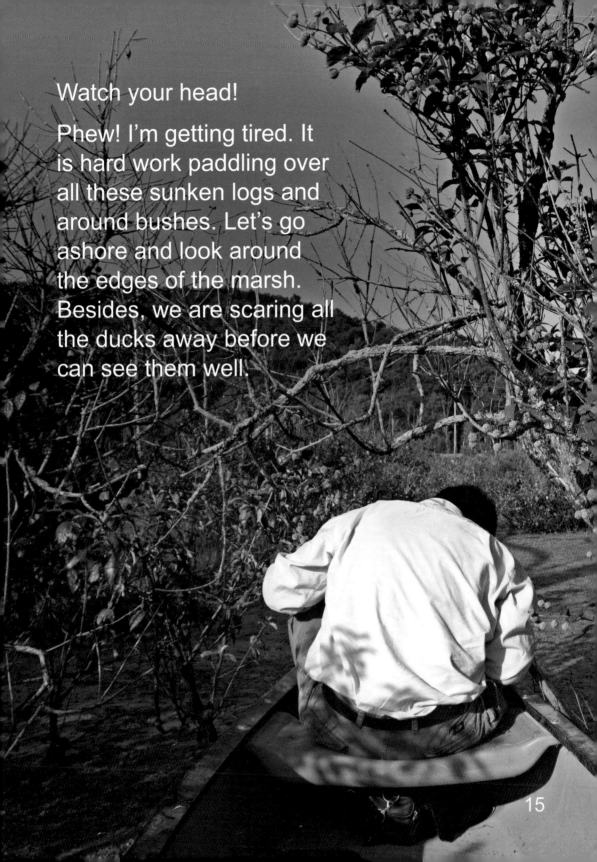

Watch your head!

Phew! I'm getting tired. It is hard work paddling over all these sunken logs and around bushes. Let's go ashore and look around the edges of the marsh. Besides, we are scaring all the ducks away before we can see them well.

15

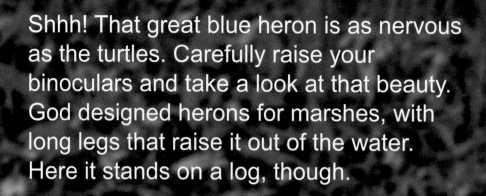

Shhh! That great blue heron is as nervous
as the turtles. Carefully raise your
binoculars and take a look at that beauty.
God designed herons for marshes, with
long legs that raise it out of the water.
Here it stands on a log, though.

When you are done watching the heron, turn your binoculars over that way to the red-winged blackbird. These birds like marshes and tall grasses.

Oh, look over there! Trumpeter swans! They are very alert, so we must stay here and use our binoculars to get a close look.

See the swan's webbed foot? It looks as big as my hand. God has given these swans big "paddles" to help them swim. About 75 years ago, fewer than 100 of these swans were known to be living. Today they number about 50,000.

Time to put away the
binoculars and get
out the magnifying
glass. This dragonfly
is a real beauty!
Approach slowly if
you want to get close.

This one is camouflaged against the background.

A sky blue tail and green eyes give this one a striking color match. God's dragonflies can fly better than man's helicopters.

Now let's watch the wood ducks. When they take off, they use their feet to help push them out of the water—almost like running on water.

When they land, they
put their feet forward
as brakes.

Can you guess why this flower is called
a broadleaf arrowhead? You will need
to look at the leaf, not the pretty white
flower, to understand.

Virginia rails usually stay hidden in the marsh grasses and reeds. To see them, you might have to call them in with a recording of their *kiddick, kiddick* call.

Psssst . . . quiet! The opossum will just walk by if we whisper and do not move. Opossums love to wander the marsh in search of something good to eat—insects, snails, snakes, mice, and maybe some small seeds or wild berries.

Let's just sit still for a while and see what else may come to eat in the marsh. While we wait, we can look at some flowers and watch for birds.

Blue vervain can
live in both swampy
and dry areas.
Although many
people consider it
to be a weed, it has
lovely violet flowers.

These bulrushes do not have brilliant flowers, but they have attractive seed heads. Moses' mother made him an ark out of bulrushes.

There goes a whitetail buck!
He does not like to wade in
swamps like moose do, but
he wanders along the edge
of the marsh. A hunter would
like to find a nice one like him
this fall.

Tall ironweed got part of its name because it can grow taller than a man. The bright flowers not only add beauty to the marsh, but also provide food for insects.

Kuk, kuk, kuk, kuk, kuk . . .

That sounds like a green heron.
There, on the dead branch! He
looks greenish when among
trees, but he really has more
rust color than green.

Though raccoons make their homes in trees, they love to hunt in marshes. They do not mind at all to get their paws wet. They use their front paws like hands to hold and wash their food before they eat it.

Raccoons look awfully cute, but they are fiesty fighters and will bite if you try to catch them.

Hidden in the middle of the water lilies is a beaver lodge built with trees the beavers cut down with their sharp front teeth. Beavers enter their house from under the water. None of their enemies can get in.

The beaver's webbed
hind feet make him
an excellent swimmer
and diver. He can
stay underwater up
to fifteen minutes!

Let's take a close look at all these damselflies around us. God dressed them in various colors.

Compare these damselflies with the dragonflies on pages 20–21. Notice the shape of the eyes and how they hold their wings while resting.

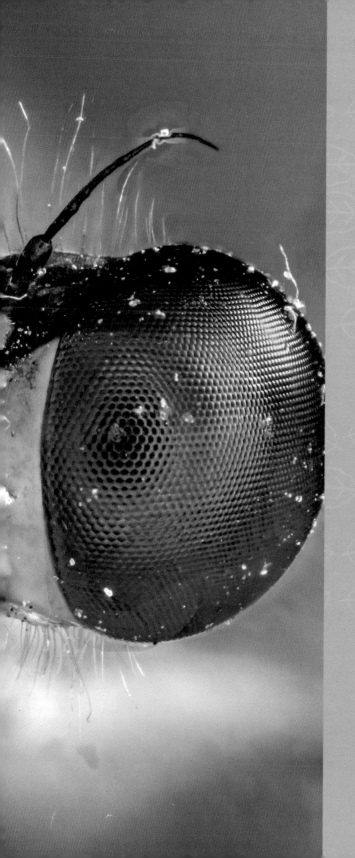

With your magnifying glass, carefully look at the damselfly's eyes.

Look at the three ocelli, the three little eyes between the two large ones.

A bald eagle! The eagle watches the marsh for prey like rabbits, snakes, fish, or other birds.

It is easy to see why this plant is called orange jewelweed. If you touch the mature seed heads, they explode and throw seeds in all directions. That is why this plant is also called touch-me-not.

Well, it is time to go. Watch your step! That little northern water snake is easy to miss. Although it is not poisonous, it can be very aggressive and act mean when cornered.

It has been a good visit to the marsh, and there is lots more we could see. Let's look at one more flower before leaving. This yellow water lily is glorifying God with its beauty, even though very few people will ever see it. Like this flower, brighten the corner where you are.

About the Author

Mike Atnip, his wife Ellen, and their son Daniel live in New Bedford, Ohio. Mike grew up among the cornfields of east-central Indiana, tromping through the fields and woods on a regular basis. Ellen grew up in southeast Pennsylvania, at the foot of Blue Mountain, but later lived in northern New York where the snow blows deep. Daniel was adopted from the tall Andes Mountains in Bolivia, South America, but has spent most of his life in the United States.

The Atnip family hopes that people young and old will see God's glory, power, and love in the creation of so many marvelous forms of life, and submit their hearts to Him as to a loving Father and Friend.

Mike welcomes reader response and can be contacted at atnips@gmail.com. You may also write to him in care of Christian Aid Ministries, P.O. Box 360, Berlin, Ohio 44610.

Christian Aid Ministries

Christian Aid Ministries was founded in 1981 as a nonprofit, tax-exempt 501(c)(3) organization. Its primary purpose is to provide a trustworthy and efficient channel for Amish, Mennonite, and other conservative Anabaptist groups and individuals to minister to physical and spiritual needs around the world. This is in response to the command ". . . do good unto all men, especially unto them who are of the household of faith" (Galatians 6:10).

Each year, CAM supporters provide approximately 15 million pounds of food, clothing, medicines, seeds, Bibles, Bible story books, and other Christian literature for needy people. Most of the aid goes to orphans and Christian families. Supporters' funds also help to clean up and rebuild for natural disaster victims, put up Gospel billboards in the U.S., support several church-planting efforts, operate two medical clinics, and provide resources for needy families to make their own living. CAM's main purposes for providing aid are to help and encourage God's people and bring the Gospel to a lost and dying world.

CAM has staff, warehouses, and distribution networks in Romania, Moldova, Ukraine, Haiti, Nicaragua, Liberia, and Israel. Aside from management, supervisory personnel, and bookkeeping operations, volunteers do most of the work at CAM locations. Each year, volunteers at our warehouses, field bases, Disaster Response Services projects, and other locations donate over 200,000 hours of work.

CAM's ultimate purpose is to glorify God and help enlarge His kingdom. ". . . whatsoever ye do, do all to the glory of God" (1 Corinthians 10:31).

Creation to Redemption

God created marshes, fish, and birds on the first five days, but animals and man on the sixth day. At first man lived in harmony with God and the earth. But after Adam and Eve sinned, some people began to worship the creation rather than the Creator. Others began to selfishly destroy the creation in their pursuit of money, pleasure, or fame.

But God sent His Son Jesus into the world to rescue us from our sin. Jesus taught us to abandon the idolatry of nature worship and to be good stewards of God's creation. He died on the cross and rose again that we could be born again and enter the kingdom of God.

This kingdom of God is made up of those who have allowed Jesus to be King of their lives. Jesus leads these people into a harmonious relationship with God and teaches them to live holy, loving, and unselfish lives as they relate to people and things on this earth. They are in the world but not of the world and look forward to their final redemption in heaven.